If (

PITT POETRY SERIES
Ed Ochester, Editor

IF ONE
OF US
SHOULD
FALL

Nicole Terez Dutton

University of Pittsburgh Press

This book is the winner of the 2011 Cave Canem Poetry Prize, selected by Patricia Smith.

Founded in 1996 by poets Toi Derricotte and Cornelius Eady, Cave Canem is a home for the many voices of African American poetry and is committed to cultivating the artistic and professional growth of African American poets.

Established in 1999, the Cave Canem Poetry Prize is awarded annually to an exceptional manuscript by an African American poet who has not yet published a full-length book of poems.

Support for the Cave Canem Poetry Prize has been provided in part by the National Endowment for the Arts and generous individual donors.

ART WORKS.
arts.gov

Published by the University of Pittsburgh Press, Pittsburgh, Pa., 15260
Copyright © 2012, Nicole Terez Dutton
Manufactured in the United States of America
Printed on acid-free paper
10 9 8 7 6 5 4 3 2 1
ISBN 13: 978-0-8229-6223-6
ISBN 10: 0-8229-6223-3

For Diana and Edward

CONTENTS

If One of Us Should Fall

GIRL #1

Girl in clear, coal-hot squares of disco, the sudden
pangs and minnowed light moving across, sloped

as candle wax and allowing such octaves
into the small thrum, her sternum, a Doppler

resonance, pleading its maps. Listen, I am girl.
Here and here. Place me

in an eyeless cornfield, not noticing the screen
door thrown wide and night coming on

like horses.

ELEMENTS

There must be a train station
never arrived at

smoky boxcar teak
and rum; a dark Jamaican

who won't say a lot. Eyes, small
dimes behind frames

furniture heavy, but attentive
to a woman

speaking in oboes, clay Florida
moons under her nails.

Think: agreement. Bouquets
beneath polyester.

And somewhere between Rochester
and Milwaukee, eyes latch

and hold. Possibly baseball
cards, a pint of Hot Damn

or cardboard towns scraping dark
landscapes by.

Think: someone nearly gorgeous.
A name without a saint. Loyal

to the Mets. (An optimist.)
Ways we fall

asleep, hands entwined. Crook
to crook, rocking. Some dreams,

they don't arrive
on the backs of tossing

ponies—but for now, everything is
beginning, the boxcar and muscular silk

against closed eyes, his sleepy
way of guessing

the number of miles by
the dust in her hair.

EVERY ANSWER IS YES

And guitars burning us up, quick
as malaria, strapped into the hind bucket
of second hand Buicks, speeding
away, always, and always dumbstruck
by the drums trundled in our bones
the whole interstate home. We love
the basement band drenching us
cottoneared. We love our pomade
and polyester bodies smashing
their atoms against other bodies,
our habit of becoming massive
bumper crops of noise. Sharpened
with sweat and honey glaze, we are
kindling, snake hips swerved to
iced Ohio hairpins, we are tucked chins
and tuned limbs set for everywhere
past curfew, past subdivision tree lawns
crackling black grackle like alarm clocks.
This blood hollers all the linking verbs
by heart, the joules inscribed within
congruent and uprising integers, the many
ways in which we are not small and not sleepy,
but born of a pure velocity. We are burning
through cassettes and frost-stunted
tulips. We love the way we carry
power chords in our teeth and wind loops
around the block with time to kill, we love
and we love, and it doesn't ever matter
if we get there.

THE KILLING WAIT FOR A TELEPHONE HELLO

In my home seven hundred miles east
of this phone booth, you spin the one
record you like best. It is good to take
Scotch slow. Etta James at age 23,
a pool hustler's unclaimed daughter,
knew the truth when she walked into the studio
and laid down tracks to her platinum
and permanently fractured heart, proving
there is reason to learn and remember
every note, to drink what burns slowly.
In my phone booth seven hundred miles
from my home, the receiver is sticky.
The ringing continues. My eyes take in tin shacks
in nattered fields, but I don't leave a message.
You will find the way, following the gandy dancer's
sweat song. The girl in the bar, beaded
like a glass bottle, skirt hitched, and his lips
on her neck making music of her while together
they dance—you will follow the midnight of that.
These are the tracks. This is the better story.
The one that wakes you up, satisfied. The place
my voice is an unnamed animal in the kingdom
of impossible things. Where Etta sings
a burn that travels a body slowly, where
everything you have is enough.

No quarters and he accepts the call. Good news
is we broke even in every club. My fingers

are callused as harvest days. Through the receiver
his laugh is work, an old dog turning circles before sleep.

I say Texas is endless, but let's agree on Soon. Don't leave
without me. I can get there by daybreak

and I will—

PLAYING THE ROOM

When it's over
they stagger from their barstools

into snow, homeward
or elsewhere, our words

in their beer, their stomachs
emptied on tree lawns,

the bed sheets twisted against,
repeated and blurry. These stray lines

sons and daughters
will catch only the weather of

behind the words,
the carcasses of steel mills

and rivers on fire. They try
to reassemble the logic the way

people interrogate suicide notes
cold trails that could lead

to the coordinates
where certain hearts lay

unspeaking, buried
in the earth like gold.

GIG

Their lives are better without you. Look
at the moon faces and raised champagne glasses
in this photograph. The dismantled flowers
on the church steps. He married
last week, and the girl, when you meet her,
is well ironed and kind. Good thing
Austin is just one in a string of occasional places.
And you, a girl with a Stratocaster growling mud
and chrome into microphones, can't stick around long.
After the set you all will be a litany of vectored facts
talking a scalloped edge around the sweet tea, six eyes
parsing the differences between then and now:
more creased, more safe, more of each of you.
What is there to speak? You are alive
within the memory of your own skin. You will be
whatever creation you choose for the onstage hour.
Eyes moldering, or not, heart lurching, or not. Tomorrow
is another town with contracts and cheese danishes.
But tonight—play them a broomjump.
Call it. Wear out. Be new.

ALMOST SONG #1

We don't know so many songs after all.

                                So, hum. (We hum.)
And the mountains
go by

*

Come to love

over time

your snoring and creaky

ankles, your teeth marks in my mind, my toast

dragged away from oncoming marmalade

or your laugh, a boxcar hobo

jumping its holy, whiskey way—

*

17 hours out

cows dip slow haunches

across the double yellow

that threadbare refrain, another town

gathered at the horizon,

a dirty hem, bad punctuation—

almost there, love

is

as specific

as I can.

Of sunnyhaired doubt: How it takes a heart down at the knees. When we look at the law we see our own distorted reflections in his mirrored glasses. We stand together examining the burgled side panel, the van window reduced to halo of glitter and crunch on the asphalt, bloody handprints on our ransacked belongings. Silence and hard Utah light rain down on us like hammers. He clears his throat finally and says: *What makes you think this was a robbery?*

He takes the report anyway. The hotel management eyes us suspicious, refuses us fresh towels while we safer hole up with spiced rum and cable television and wait until the replacement van window installation can get us gone.

Days later, safe in Arizona, the law calls saying they found your amplifier, other stolen odds and ends. *Come on back and get it.*

We do not return the precinct telephone call. We cash the insurance check, order thick roadside diner steaks and cold beer. We eat surrounded by red rock and other dark and canyon featured ones, safe finally, safe with people in from hawking dream catchers on the shoulder, their clay ramshackles lining the interstate like molars.

We do not smile or talk but linger over our plates, watch basketball on the TV, then the news, and whatever comes after news until closing. Outside, many sunless miles snake the mountains and subsequent foothills into Texas. The close air of our stepping, our hackles up and bellies full, that mysterious unspoken, fried up in the ink and pauses, the screen door banging softly behind us, a one handed drum. Holding us, this away.

VERTICAL HOLD

Fall radio silent, into the traffic
of variables working themselves around
the fact of your head. After surgery
he does not want to come back. Everybody says
Go There, says *Sorry.* You damn well know
your grandfather's bedside awaits.
His brogans stalled on the back stairs, his margins
overrun with handwriting. Their mouths
stitch themselves around the question *When?*
You are on the way, your body crackling
with the static of Pennsylvania electrical storms.
Cows pin down the acreage with indifferent hooves
and your car is overrun with guitars,
with sad boy voices, sad leather
boys with hair drizzled down their backs,
boys pretty enough sing loose the rusty irons
through the waxen wrists of Jesus statues.
Harmonies loop and reel against bait shacks
and strip malls until Delaware falls away,
a three syllable scab lost to weather, until Virginia's
slow farmhouses curtsey and go. Until you stop
for coffee and push the tractor trailers around the plate
with your fork. Keep your blood threaded
with sugar and tail lights blooming down the coastline
until you can fall without considering the mechanics
of impact, fall in the angle his cursive leans, fall
as if darkness can be pulled back in sheaves
and dropped into, a distance whittled by careful
instruments and determination, a thing to be held
in both hands. Fall until you can land needle clean,
until you can be streamlined, the dark name carved
into the tree of his heart.

THE CITY WHERE

Was narcotic, always is
the breakneck and leaving,

our bodies, lean
and strange, from one

to the next, gone.
This is how

good stories are made
to crawl from skin, to snake

the hips like interstate,
to tug and swallow that music

whole. Halfway in
the syntax of the country

falls down. Turns out
our dictionaries are wrong

Turns out we are not at all
what we expect.

Each song a city best arrived at
empty, a place to keep snow

in slow motion falling,
falling forever, the last

people we used to know.

MINOR KEY

Thumb and lobe, so tiny
a beginning—a mind gone

blank as milk while in back
they dozed and mountains shrank

to fog in the rearview. Tomorrow
is a tavern thick with pig feet

and guitars, a sticky hour built
for beer and bodies in sway.

Time swallows itself. We will
begin slow and tell the truth. Tomorrow

a world, ten fingers less, will move
forward. There will be more

soldered wires, more chords and flesh
held closed with butterfly clamps.

For now, there are three aspirin
and a place to lay it down, the Grand Tetons

in endless retreat, bring
their granite stillness into greenrooms,

and booth vinyl, some moment
between ribs and paychecks,

where hale voices fortified by notions
and potatoes find time to sleep.

We will sleep. We will remain strangers
and no one by looking could know

what parts have gone missing. We will arrive
in Austin where the men wear belt buckles

the size of license plates and smile at us
like they mean it, they keep us

believing there is always somewhere else
to arrive, house lights to dim, second chances,

another day.

ALMOST LULLABY #1

Sleep? I tip
as if felled.
Sky, a slow-motion crinoline.
I am the pivot point,
the ballerina's toe gnarled beneath the twirling.

Close your eyes.
it doesn't matter who holds
the whip or where

welts begin—

the dance floor, empty
and ale-sticky before the thundering
of Stetsons, anonymous
motel rooms honeycombed around
steakhouses and highway
ramps.

Close your eyes.
There are so many bar chords
up and down the neck—

strum.

*

I love
your earth-
colored eyes waiting
for a beat

to break
into, the silence
around silence,
within small hours

the way your voice
is so close to my ears
while outside
the Texas sky
opens and opens,
where the ground leaps up
to catch fat medallions of rain.

CHASER

You are almost dying, smooth
thin wrists, all the time. This is
what waiting does. By the time
the voice on the telephone
arrives at *you are too good,*
to keep your guts have packed out,
eyes gone hollow as Penn Station
without wingtip hurry, a thousand umbrellas
deftly shaken free of rain. You are
fingers run across, slide hollow
scraped up the neck, you are
practice.

Lying is many scavenger birds, knees
beneath dinner tables
crossed and uncrossed, a virus
fortressed in blood and spit,
a name you do not speak,
feathers left in the mouth.

And now you belong
to the long pause on the answering machine
after the beep, the moment
in which countless trees went flying by,
squat railside tenements
threaded with backyard laundry,
scrolled blue as ghost
in that twilight spring
hello—

The pause is an oncoming answer.
The pause is nothing you don't already know.

This evening birds might
festoon the trees. Jays, thuggish,
brazen. You will want to kill them
to stop their shrieking,
but will climb the fire
escape and watch a moon rise
red as disaster,
a decapitated horse head
lobbed into the sky
barking to the birds
shut up
shut up.

ON THE WAY

I have decided and redecided
a few times before she comes
squeaking back with coffee, the pitcher
of cream. I love she calls me *Hon*
and reassures *Take your time.* Twelve hours
to Ohio and rain, a hard static
I've been pretending to decipher
won't let up. I pick the broken line
from the radio, news, sports—
more squawk and banter until
my cup runs empty. Time's short
but I had to pull over. Get out.
Slink a little through the bells at the
front door and slide into a booth
to watch the rain beat the road down.
She appears out of nowhere,
smiling. Eggs and coffee. *Hon.*
You're almost there.

We can only sing razorblades over the brim of Nashville. Can only permit the fiddle to scrape against something familiar in our blood, to rise all ghosts to the surface, and call our names from the hushed canebrake beyond the gas station's sad halo of light. Some places need to be traveled through. We know that language won't survive past Ohio. That we will fall fast and out of time. The fracture will be exquisite. Soy fields and early frost whipping by is what we have. A few hours, and the urge to punch it down to the floorboards, to let those horses out. These gorgeous miles raced alongside—all of us, pretending to dream.

SUNLIGHT

How I carry
You:

radiant from the sternum,
breath flared with whiskey

close to the ears

a body
spoken across

cobbled and sleepyheaded cities
a prime number moving

toward airplanes, dogwood trees;
this is how
I carry your words

against my skin,
the pelt of a living animal

the weight of a man
stripped of body, of bone.

TOURISTS #1: APPROACHING GLORIETTE AT SCHÖNBRUNN PALACE, VIENNA

The museum is an imperial 1,441-room rococo summer palace, and the palace is sprawled like someone thrown headlong from the heavens into lush Viennese countryside. Schönbrunn Palace is in fetal position, cheek in the dirt, and has been for the past three hundred years. Begonias fatly clump at the lip of the stairwell and the stairwell is a marble sneer bringing us into another badly lit rotunda, a rotunda exquisitely throttled with portraits of the Habsburg family. We have elected against the tour. Our legs are tired from wandering the hedge mazes and reflecting pools. The statues are Greek tragedies. Several marble depictions of Zeus pitching his thunderbolts remind us that passion is worth celebrating. To live greatly and within striking distance of flawed and partial gods is to move properly within these families of married cousins. The smell of powdered flesh beneath an unwashed corset mingling with the champion roses. How we flock to see it. Horsehair wigs and wooden teeth on china at tea hour. We eat sandwiches by the fountain where mermaids spit swales of water fifteen feet in the air. Alabaster cupids piss endless arcs. Just meters from where they decided the fate of the kingdom, dusted and unsmiling, in a place without mirrors or a single shaft of direct sunlight.

We keep pace and exchange verbs, ideas handsomely placed beneath the creases of a larger circumstance. But we must be going, always. Must sample local pastries and count correct change in the foreign coin. We move through other slow museum watchers. It takes patience to navigate. Thank God we love poetry! That parade of strange, proofless animals. We can absorb the vegetable silences behind the curtains of restored palaces and on wide cathedral steps. Thank God the watchers agree to agree. Some of us, ensconced in pages and concertina piano chords, some of us, in slow flannel mornings, rising with breadcrumbs in our beards and the rind of whatever moon staled within our paper wasp mouths while we searched for our brushes and nouns—some of us do not feel like our familiar selves. We are houses filled with someone else's furniture. Sad photocopies with fuzzled edges and approximate hands. Within those first moments of wakefulness we address the sunlight in a stranger's body, rise on sore knees, hungry for certain voices, the salt of specific skin. There are people we are born missing, their faces in a field just beyond, and fractures so compounded that we take ourselves across oceans, live off the bread and coffee, move like sleepwalkers toward the next gallery. The paintings do not look familiar, but the faces may resemble ones we used to know, those deliberate gestures and inventories, and perhaps we cross oceans to recognize them. Thank God someone told us to pay attention. To mark these locations on our maps and in notebooks. To stand with the sea writhing in all directions in a field of fiercely bright azaleas, ready, alongside everything else, to burn.

WHERE SLEEP CANNOT

You have many times been
the hand-carved maple bowl,
useful, with dark grain, or small
plum, flesh against teeth, a fact
like hunger or weather, misread
tea leaves, good medicine, a canyon
opening silence more deeply. You have been
brass, breathed into. You have been
expanded with time and heat, the narrow
vowel within the five plotlines
mapping a closed fist, the shattered picture
window. Without question you've been
the shard, its bright music, a body gouged
to the point of flowers, heaving. Years
you were miscellaneous keys, chores
undertaken, a monk's thin gruel. And, this:
someone's missing pearls, someone's
hard frost and busted pipes,
a morning ransacked by garbage trucks,
or elevator between floors, sore-kneed
apology, moment of nakedness halfway
across a bridge or stage, a name
on a tongue in a head where sleep cannot
find you, that bright ache or spoonful
of ashes, that field of tall grass beneath
an ocean of fireflies, the place returned to
always better than just good enough
that one promise kept, the only reason why.

1. [phenomenon] The redacted "unreasonable." The manner in which eyebrows vault skyward in disbelief, or in which a knife cleanly slid over flesh becomes tart, uncomplicated language; the sweep of shoreline in repose, a face over coffee or open ocean dreaming in sifted gold. Any shoreline. Any dark interior. Landscape rich with the suggestion of further sky and highways welting vast stretches of wilderness. The price of passage. The hunger to go.

2. [phenomenon] Gangster syndicate with Queen's orders, fluent pox like English. The cavalcade movement of men, women and children upon the shores and fanning out. The God upon their tongue a lead bullet, a fever, a willfully dismantled village, people, tradition, language or landscape.

3. [direction] Sunset driven into, minivan with socks; unshaven sleepiness and the narrow sprawl of club dates from coast to coast, series of sad motels in pastel disrepair, handfuls of telephone quarters, guitars that call us by the names our mothers gave, the body as cathedral of many chambered noise

4. [symbol] Covered wagon. Puritan cornucopia of savage fruit and gizzards, full-throttle stallions lathered toward El Dorado. Horizon overbrimming velvet saloon bustier and dust covered whiskey tin. Plague of little post-prairie prairie houses. Compulsory Carolina exodus parade from mangrove to dustbowl. Compulsory school bus echo. The whitewater river running through it. Klan hand-blasted visage of four dead presidents in the mountains of promised land.

5. [phenomenon] The production of ghosted landscape, the shackle music and weight upon bones, the sick pitch of the full-bellied

boat; God of speed toward another coast, a place more closely resembling the end of the world.

6. [phenomenon] Restlessness of spirit. Open sky opening. Land far and beyond the proportion of personal otherhood. Orchestration without time signature. Towns shunk down to past tense on the horizon. Hysteria dressed in the flames of dying maple and momentum, strings vibrating against a landscape without buffalo, red wolf, short-necked Chicksaw ponies, bees, barley. It is a big sound, the heart tumbling around cold water tenements and canyons, the rusted-down bottling plant, fallow malls, sleepy costal towns after the seasonal parade of detritus and corn dogs, the thoroughfare abandoned, fewer daylight hours lapping against night.

7. [phenomenon] Tripping. Police on the highway flagging down the suspicious. Convenient and aggressively vague definition of suspicious. A prison sentence without charge, without trial, without term. A habit of disappearing all squeaky wheels, encouragement toward silence. Offering a mutable dictionary. A night seared by sirens, a moment shrunken to a noose. A voice that replaces one's own, and stepping from the crushed throat into bright air, strains its verbs against 20 uniformed bodies of *Hell no.*

8. [phenomenon] The making of exquisite noise. The survival of genius. Genius transmission via underlanguage, overtongue, intersong, transhamonic polymorphorhythm, visual drumbeat, quilted scrapings, adornment, basket grass, indigo stained palm, spice, hidden alphabet, dance, constant agitation, sweet hurricane of song.

9. [location] Geographical location famous for promise of gold. A direction less than one hundred years from where young girls stand in dresses the color of faded everything, bonnets and skirts, like bells filled with wind. Fields that become dustbin to bigger ideas, squat towns thrown like a poker dice, space between them scarred with rails. The unmarked grave and pogrom latitude. Territory upon which whole towns were swallowed by fire. Where men shoot at bison from the windows of passing trains, the place where they fall and fall.

10. [interrogative] The multiplicity of questions. Can you? Jag a little music there; make it all the way to ocean. Move steadily without expanding with possession; without becoming full as a tick; a hide wasted in prairie wheat, swollen cumulous of flies. Can you read the winds and their constant shifting. Learn the ghosts in every landscape. Remember their names. Know where you are.

DESOLATE

Des [traditional] name for the first born daughter + Sola [traditional]
    the curved heel on a black leather shoe specific to fado
b. Kisi clan female name meaning, "She for whom time arrives
    stillborn"

Des [obsolete] the first beat of desire. Quick blood.
A thick vein of black oil flooding through Arctic frost, her voice.
An apricot or ocean. Body past dark in fields of wet tobacco.
Or "almost there, a path prepared."
One who makes turning a corner possible.
Rain. Small pieces of light.

La [rare] the abbreviated form of Lola (the woman in a song he of-
ten thought he saw reading magazines on trains dense with breath-
fogged windows and the wet wool of strangers; a woman to whom
he found himself in close enough proximity to notice the spill of
freckles galloping in unrecognizable patterns down her neck and
wonder *What galaxy is this?* A woman with whom he would never
have conversation, a woman, therefore, perfect, and permanently on
her way elsewhere, him, hovering at the periphery, therefore, perfect
in his loving, the heat from her neck, the dim lavender of her hair.)

Late [origin unknown] spice indigenous to grasslands and temper-
ate climes traditionally used to cure meats. Word meaning *tasting
of copper.* Referring to specific systems and relationships of nuclear
objects, e.g., the way his silk dress shirt hangs ironed in the closet.
The star formation in which the board members invariably assemble
around the mahogany table, the act of ignoring one empty chair, the
deliberate, unchased bourbon, pork chops with mint jelly, the best
friend and his heavy shoes headed homeward, the wife whose body
is a paper birch canoe, famous for its hollowness, the eagerness with

which other people speak into her to hear the resonance of their own spoken name, the way she sat by the bedside as if at any moment he might rise from the dreams of bracken and slippery elm like before, hungry from his wandering, like before, his quick smile a ready indication that he was ready to go home.

THE YOU IN THIS POEM

Doesn't have to
try hard to be the one

raw with trumpets and lightning broken
across a crowded room—

something we all are
brighter and suddenly foreign for,

as if we'd forgotten,
the archipelago of our bodies

or the salt in all directions
calling out our name.

The you in this poem
doesn't so much speak as stir

a darkness of loosened feathers,
claws and tendriled weather

upon our eyes and open mouths.
No telling why the music carries,

or what might pry the ribs open.
I'm not sure which equation

might rescue you from your own skin—
I'm saying I like sky when you speak it.

I'll never care which latitude,
even if you leave your body

by the roadside for the crickets—
I'll recognize the spine bowed

as Herodotus beneath its story,
the sore knees, the bruised and perfect

mouth. I know just how to find you
no matter what the distance, I'll hear

the pastures singing back our voices,
a blade of grass for every tongue.

NIGHT

Thank you for looking away, please leave me
right here. My cobbled tongue, poor excuses.

I don't need to see
that animal at all. Thank you

for this slow train on its way. Thank you
for a place bottomless enough

to bring my imploded head. Thank you
for not looking, for your eyes sewn like buttonholes,

for your voice like a blanket of thumbs,
for not missing all lost things equally,

even the fingerprints long since rubbed off
on the inside of my mouth.

OUTSKIRTS

Lights wink off
from blue hillsides.

This night comes on slow
horses. The hollowbody

leaned into while we wait
for the train, these past few

days without umbrellas,
some singing, the place

we leave off: dim oranges,
risen moon.

PHOTOGRAPH WITH UNNAMEABLE GIRL

Tucked into a book, a sepia photograph
with scalloped edges. A girl with coal eyes
chipped against oiled valves, the engine
darkly revving inside his chest or long shadow,
an unfamiliar tautness to his jaw,
the smile's thin grip on his face. We know this
story: the sift and crackle of paper wrappers,
wind in the streets after carnival, a starved dog
all night scratching an unopened back door.
Creased village women, without coffee for weeks,
gunfire above clay rooftops,
or goat roasted over open fire, the day
before the first day without her, the girl, the two
crow-hard eyes like a pair of unlucky dice, patched
suitcase and a ticket on the roadside beside him,
a name ungiven, a face unknown.

QUOTIDIAN

Days longhand 22 hours
trenchless sunshine, ABBA,
war, our wince over eggs
or chorus with Muddy—
no matter what
longitude
we're always laundry
for the way we might
sing along, a coffee cup
in the window, *Go then*—
and you rise
and squall
through the streets
half mad for the bones
of her face, knowing
no one can be
hurried toward, approached
except with delicacy.
At the corner
you stop and wait,
let the heat press
into your skin
as if her breath
were sunlight.

SEVERAL BLUE AND POSSIBLE ENVELOPES

We wandered until we found vacancy.
Details without calculus. I thought

to send a letter, imagined my voice
a slim blue envelope

beside your coffee cup—but no.
My sugarfoot and suitcase, the whole day

frittered to sundown or tourist
districts. I understand motion

sickness and must stop
often alongside rusty canals

to think of other possible blue
envelopes, powder blue hello waving,

or photographs showing a little brass,
that yellow scarf in the corner of the frame.

The exact silk you gave me. Embroidery
too small to see.

TOUCH

It ends at airport pizza.
Full stop with terrorists' threats
some ornamentalist discussion

rooted in nevermind
my emphatic
if we blow up, we blow up.

This small day, your power
is to choose the last photograph, cherry cola
or peanuts, your angle of recline.

I chose
Vienna. Those pews.
Candle wax sloped with hush

and strangers
in from four corners of gray rain.
The frankincense and pine

we slid into,
sitting, rising, kneeling
Catholic, our necks

bent the path Jesus stumbled
toward saints. Your breathing
beside me, wet jeans

thighs almost
close enough
to touch.

103 and unrisen. Brine beneath sleep,
bed sheets rumpled and damp. In these hours
before dawn, in the comfortable hum
of everybody home, the house spells out
its own dreams rich with mice and splinters,
unmatched socks, frosting. Everything curves
to the hand it holds or that holds it, knobs latch,
stairs bow with their honest and familiar burdens,
and within layers of milk paint
you smell like ocean. I sing every song I know.
I call your name three times softly. *You are mine.*
You are mine. You are mine.

SLEEP IS NOT OUR COUNTRY

Night foxes in wet grass wreathe
my house with hunger. A slight

figure against the green
foothills, I rise early

and accompany the miles
into dawn. The hills ahead

hold him, sleepless, too. His voice,
medicine, soft animal. Each

step behind us
veined with cool water

or crow etched into pale
sky. This is the way

the body sings
exhaustion or promise:

notes from an opened throat
rising, space hurtled through,

until we can only imagine
who we might have been,

until even our own fingers
run along the creases

and bindings of our odd and perfect
dimensions are new.

Even hog-tied in telephone wire and bleached beyond stars, I love that sky the whole way down. This is New York, grainy black-and-white film; every piece of light singing to the point of static. New York in the days spent sorting archival correspondence run with silverfish. My mouth is crammed with impeccable handwriting. You are alive. Our voices still bright with puppies, rushing past bodega jackfruit and bean pie. We are going to a party and decide on the electric-blue hydrangeas—a snowcone of tiny flowers carried like a torch through a crowd streaming from the subway's mouth. There are trees on the way and you say *Sit down. Let's build a better story. Forget the clockface for a moment, I'd just like to know.* Those trees are sudden with their crickets. Streetlight distorts to fever pitch, a blizzard of grain across the curve of your slow eyes. Behind us a three-story tenement thrums air conditioning and timbales. Streetlight pools in your cuffs and blue jeans, but never makes it past the hydrangeas in your hand. We are at such heights, I hadn't noticed. I see nothing but sky here, papyrus beneath a well dressed sentence. And you, suddenly without shadows, without silverfish in your hair.

STARLIGHT, ELSEWHERE

Hunger is an old story, a threadbare afternoon,
torn open as if by mice in the bones of a cold house.

The family, that weird station, that series of events—
we will never be enough. Kick yourself off

on another adventure. Whatever story you need
can shout itself loudest over the gutted rooms.

This is not fate, this is firewood. You are not lost,
you are transposed—you are starlight, elsewhere,

someone's grass-stained child overrun
with rain, a taste of bitterness. Your red mouth

and weak eyes. You are not gone, not vanished,
you are flying, hair blown back,

and in this posture, this constant motion, look
how suddenly you belong. How old circumstances

fit you like bad shoes, same as anyone.
Even before you reach the pier, it is plain

sky broke its promises and crumbled into sea.
How light becomes a kingdom of salt. How the sea

continues, restless and tossing. Your name within it,
a small muscle, a smooth and silent stone.

THINGS THAT WILL NOT FORGET US

Only certain facts piston the heart
double time. Cistern water swirls

clockwise, sinks sweetly into loam.
What is necessary is easily recognized

by its absence, these mid-sentence exits,
the sense that everything was fine until it wasn't.

Each face at the table swears on a different
version. We consult the family Bible for the names,

the pages smelling of other spring times,
when the river breached the dyke, filled the first

floor, and felled trees too young too soon. A house
never recovers, never becomes the same house.

The boy grows into a man whose horsehair bow
thickens with resin, a man whose Mozart

sings like reeds disturbed by increasing
wind, gray waves licking up, a town ready

to pack out. Even years after the blood ends,
the building holds itself together like a sigh, the rooms

await the return of something. The slaughterhouse
remembers the last of the hooves and knee bones,

the squealing even dim animals are born capable of,
the gleam of the knife, the blessing sharpness of the blade.

CITY OF CANDY-COLORED LIGHT

Hope makes us strange and hope makes us kin.
By the nose into negative red, we go, four bodies
rich with mosquitoes and poison oak, sleep unslept
staining our sockets and mouths. We follow the queen
into this corpus of gin and dice exploded against
felt. Collect the clubs and diamonds, acquire a vigilance
for triple cherries after midnight. We sit down and learn.
On the left Mutton Chops battles Lucky Strike. Prom Queen,
equipped with fanny pack and Chivas neat, is a Jedi
with her cards. Her spine, sore from honest work,
is a regal collapsing thing. And while the chips raise their towers
of possibility, she will count the dollars, make preparations
for the long ride home with a radio between stations. One hour
outside city limits radio waves thin to salt flats and starlight.
We're headed that way. We've been where night grows
its miles, where the sky kneels down and the horizon flares
all directions. We like the sound of it. The quiet that closes
around us, the music that swallows us whole.

MANY KINGDOMS TOWARD YOU

The map in yesterday's suitcase, a river
whose name dropped vowels and feathers

in its hurry to bring us here, notes
eased from an old piano, flowers

touching down—so quiet a way
of speaking this country of wire

and silver bone. Somewhere a forest
enlarged with moonlight, weeping

what hands could not hold, waits.
It is snow, a way of speaking

many flowers at once. This silk
or sky, gathered dogwood

at great distances. The way your eyes
are snowing, always, many kingdoms

spoken at once, stillness
I avalanche toward.

Let's keep the billboards as witness and benchmark
for miles through sly time zones slyly gone,
all the weird circumstances passing for music
between and during the occasions we find ourselves on stage.
It does not matter the direction of our rambling. Our
days map the intersection of four relatively unacquainted lives.
This is where we are. We belong to each other and nowhere
else. Dark stones dropped into the glassy center, we are
accustomed to the way eyes stampede across our faces
the terrible silence behind certain words. This is far from home,
where we fall in love with twilight, with leaving. Where we
find an orchard and spread ourselves like paper dolls in the
grass. It is easy to fall past the cherry blossoms into basins
of starlight, to think that in time reason will come to us,
if we stay together and keep moving, making noise
out of the empires of dead light our eyes only now can see.

More details stretch the canvas, our bright and hurried patches of telephone conversation. There is a new object: By Louisiana all roads taper to a single bridge overlooking alligator glades. Police pulled a man from his car, flung him across the hood like laundry. The traffic surged past, a long parade of non-looking. His head opened somewhere around the eye. A stain spread it's low red. Keep it going. Nothing to see here. One smashed a gloved hand on our hood and waved us forward. You are listening. Light crumples like wax, a cruel weight kneeling among the azaleas. Dark wings gather in the trees beyond the phone booth, notes spill from their oiled throats. The rain is slow and steady, a color you already know.

In my photographs you are always 42, solid redwood and laughing. A carnival of hand-me-down stories, such good animals, and our faces worn out, smiling. People in the street remember when. The heart didn't burst, but filled and filled. The way afternoon turns and gallops into empires of crystallized light. There is always more, a next thing, another act. Always a moment where your shoulders broadly pivot. One last slow dance before the lights come up: it is agreed. And we are again another two among the pairings, harmonized feet and jokes.

I keep a space between my ribs for your matchbooks and unabridged dictionaries, the dark-eyed row houses with overgrown rosebushes, herbs savaged by squirrels, stunted by too much cold. A place large enough to hold lake effect weather, whistled concertos, stories your mother told you. You have a moment for rainwater to wring from my hem and tangles; time to curl around my sleep. You are 42 years old. You will always be so. Will always be the last sigh before sidewalks empty, the familiar emptiness of airports, a train nosing away. You are well missed. Your breath corrals my ears, studs its way down to bone.

ALMOST NOTE #3

Vase etched with delphinium
next to the bed. The flowers
keel over. Leave them, you insist.
Muted television flickers
the *Wheel of Fortune. The Price
is Right.* They clap and kiss on his
and hers jet skis. Settle in. I am
at your side, slow as Sunday,
waiting for the next thing that might
happen along.

ANTECHAMBER

We cannot undo
the hot throated shock of azaleas,

familiar streets that open empty
as licked skillets to frail light, or speech

in its soft, old shoes
every speckled, blue morning since.

Leave off with the saying, then. Each
syllable exhausting, a stage prop, recognizable

from cheap seats. We know
what this means.

There is a moment bodies drop
from the orbit of each other,

the miles unravel. It takes only a second.
The hungers, the buttonholes,

that once precious *Stay*. Not everything
capable of brightness, can, in fact, burn.

Winter showed up suddenly,
replaced all air in the city

with hard light, slowed all frames to still.
A stark pair of wings carve an arc

into sky above the pond, as if to say
we know what we know.

This is inaccurate, but before I could
argue the wings carried themselves away.

Please recall the idea of progress. The way
one arrives in certain stanzas,

or in which wars continue, mortar
and accords signaling nothing.

The earth balds beneath such waltzing,
sick with fish and honeybees unable

to find their way home. Sometimes,
we have company, words

to be lost within, a trusty skull
rerunning its hallelujahs,

night air on upturned lapels, the few minor characters
loved well enough to bury in ink.

(Let's say I'm saying *When I love you I am admiring the fingerprints of every hand that has touched you.* Time is radiant. Vectored in all directions. And the larger issue is a little regard for straight lines. Breath coming into this idea deeper than ice age. Pushes against the same molecules. Even my saying it alters the speed light takes to reach your retina, reverses and reverses again my dimensions before you. It is dynamic, this now: We touch and touch and touch. This being again my voice, speaking into the cool green where fog sets its soft weight, my voice again asking the switchbacks: *Which syllable is not daylight? Which syllable is sleep?*)

LANDSCAPE WHILE WAITING

You are here. My whole life
hopscotched above graveyards.
Tall grass hissed though, ammunition
sipped past poison or cocktail olives
rough in the air around my wrists
and ankles. I am here. God is not proven,
but certainly, friend, your heart slamming
its doors against my half-awake listening,
blood-fist to opened flower—certainly
we know something of Grace,
having watched night deepen together,
without speaking, our hair entwined.

In the nick of school busses, office slacks, the rest of the game: Welcome Home, Girl. Critical objects to fragment and pony, sure—but I got this soft-shoe double step down. Books all memorized. You rolled some tardy and went fish-eyed in the cut: a tired, trifling air-kiss bye-bye. But that's the providence of maybe. The jokes have teeth, so I'm rocking my apples on home. My flunked cadenzas, and reasons why not—we're tripping the Fung Wah back to gasoline shingled grown folk talk and late night Stella with Isaac drunk on Jesus and hollering pulled-pork televisions—the last real place known. Cops steady taking turns taking us out, protocol spreading countless eagles across the hoods of America. Nevermind holding anything said or done against—I'm going back, argyle over Crunk, more transmorphography than any flavor hyphenation ever learned me. Just mighty lock and pop of hammer shanks and cornrow. 400,000 verbs banging like nobody's br'er told you so. That's razzle-dazzle, kid. Gold standard sonnets and shit. Just like old heads gospelizing on the stoop. Like backbeat beating. Youngins dealing hand-me-down jokes and ball. Same stories. Musicianeers. Mojomen. Mamis. Gonna be. Serious. Breaking down another dawn. Shout lovely, black! Home like *sweet* and *thank you, honey.* Damn.

ON HOLIDAY

Your ribs were carried off, perhaps
toward Namibia, you thought. It was very unclear.

The water was narcotic. It blew your ears out
like cheap speakers and left your brain

rattling its tin. At one point you were sure
you heard the streets of Mindelo hushed

with fado dancers, soft black shoes and hundreds
of girls twirling clockwise. Then the waves deepened,

moved slower and the shoreline disappeared.
Your friends were not thinking of you. Stuffed

with ham sandwiches and red juice, they were sleepy
and glazed in coconut oil. They were going to burn.

You were not thinking of them either. You were
halfway to Namibia. From the muscled water you called

but the words pelted your face like wedding rice.
So you stopped, let your arms go cast iron heavy

in the salt. Eventually you climbed ashore. Sharp rocks
opened your soles and you understood your weight as more

than just thrashing. Your friends beneath their umbrella
did not awaken when you retuned—and you will not want

to mention any of this—not over vodka
that night or dueling guitars the next. You will want

to pack your luggage and kiss their scorched cheeks.
You will want something to carry your body

in the direction of home, to simply go.

DEVOTED

Familiar, then
with dim voltage, the rain
or shine crew stitched
into daylight and savings,
any odd number of right
angled tragedies, really, flood
the train, dry erasing
our vistas, our bloom-
ing succession of taxis,
and neckties—

Still I cannot rally
albino conversation
into steak and potatoes.
Cannot crack
into private
smiles, my war chest of sugars,
promises sardineing
into leases—I will be
raining babies!
Jump the dumb turnstile,
damn Yankee swaps.

*

Regardless, a galaxy of sprockets
and kickshaw bricolage swell
from my Stratocaster and, therefore,
me. Tell my mother
I need help with the plane ticket.
Tell my mother my pockets are crammed
with postcards and whalebone. When I fall

asleep on the train it is always the same
dream: a battalion of hummingbirds
fluttered within my rib cage.
I always awaken too soon. It is always Pennsylvania,
the doors of my jacket thrown open
an epidemic of wings
released and long gone.

*

There is a keening for land, the rock
of winter that sharpens and slays us,

an unpadded cell for the tantrum
that has misplaced its alphabet.

*

Winter is happening, immediately.
My pants drag their salt-stained
scruff around town and, therefore,
me. Certainly I will meet Carla
at the bar. Bass notes may threaten
to pop the buttons off my shirt and rain
like dark tears into someone's beer. I am
beyond palms crushing out applause;
transfixed by Guilatti at the drum set,
all brushes and overtones glancing
off my teeth—listen to those
sparks, the fearless prow beneath the sizzling stars,
how he ploughs ahead.
No change.

No thanks.
No taxis after 3 am.

*

Whatever I say
licks its knots and pitches
itself over the telephone wire
a haphazard movement
against the balance of blue sky,
absentia, aluminum siding, chain link,
concrete—everything
turns clockwise and clockwise before deep sleep.

*

Something fossilizes in the third lobe, its scales
melted by rain or wind. A little wing flung to the dirt
without singing. The sky that lost it, looking on.

*

If this were a painting, the clouds would be
slung low. It would be a Pennsylvania,
windy barns, horses,
wobbling fences with open gates
but mostly, sky
an oil paint thick as clay
over which we could run our fingers
a reminding: whichever direction we cast our gaze—
space we cannot fill, space we cannot leave.

YOU AND I HERE

None too fancy, I love
the tweed of good spectacle. True,

the collective gaze is better suffered
with whiskey, in rooms cowed by famosos

speaking 100 percent calligraphy—
but enough's enough. The words,

blown glass apples, pockets of light
trapped within cool, untasting freight:

Beautiful. It is not unkindness, this crop,
but a species of forgetting. A repetitive injury

that withers the mechanics of *I'm listening.*
(I'm listening with all my scraping hooves

and sea sickened nostrils, the entire weary ark
of my distractions, all the starving and heartbreak

and dying that goes on in within
each wooden, pitching Now.) Why varnish alone?

Gesture is not cathedral. Cathedral is the moment
the body flies beyond its dirty brogans. It is bus fare

and sky beyond all wingspan, certain details
of importance, for example, you here and I here—

the great, naked kingdom of that.

He loaded the film the way he does everything:
fast, confident, almost right. The sprockets never
caught. He took at least 100 photos
before admitting this. The admission, too:
fast, confident, almost right. The photographs
would be as follows: a pink sky, settled
on cool haunches, stones and seaweed spread
in vague constellation. Contrails spiraling and draped
across the beach, something to be swallowed
with the last of the beer. Dunes broken
like waves in freefall. The unpaved service road
wheel-churned plumes of sand. In these photographs
the sky is always robin's-egg blue, the beach house is
somberly shuttered. The vetoed passage I wrote
for the guestbook is something I transcribe into my
notebook in print neat and orderly as baby teeth.
The dog, bitterly sick from seawater, hangs a heavy
head over my arm, which, like the rest of my body,
has been clipped from the frame. The frame is focused
exclusively on the sculpture of passage, the dunes' muscular
expanse, a place we will not return to, a tide
just beginning to come in.

FLEDGLING

1.

A season of blood poison and rain. Outside, pregnancy.
I should be sleeping. Eating flax seeds and broccoli,
gathering music within my husks and binds,
something that will wrench itself from the body
in its own time. Something that needs to split you in two
in order to taste the air for itself.

2.

Word on the street slings its overbright colors. I saw your bike
hurtling toward dim lace, a pair of eyes inching up
the spine of another mistake, hips thick as chilled vodka, eyes
rimmed. She is not home. Packed and gone. I came across her silk
scarves in the resell. Our rainsoaked, crowding three
asking the consignment girl
to sell it for us, her narrow empire
of secondhand nil.

3.

Your thoughtful questions: *Don't you know
that Providence is locked after eleven o'clock
and no sushi anywhere?*

I know
many ways to starve.

Make it out alive?

I danced the whole way.

Friday was canceled, so I got in the car and drove into this snowbank. Snow, then gravel hissed up from back tires spun nearly bald. Valiant efforts were made. Just around the corner, your lights were on. I won't be a minute I promised myself. I'll make quick apologies for the surprise, for questions answered slant, the indoor/outdoor carpeting darkened with slush from my boot teeth: I need your phone. And to stand here in rock salt eaten mittens while the AAA phone line sings smooth jazz. The reason is obvious. Heat makes a burden of layers and tomorrow will be sore in the hips and quads. Still, blizzards improve every city: Strangers talk to strangers and make deals like *Share*. Or *You dig, I push* and cars across the zip code lurch themselves free. Heading into dark, bundled beyond good sense, we're going to try this and fail. Shoulder to shoulder is progress, but eventually we tire. Eventually your mouth suggests *Put away the shovels and leave the car in the ditch for a while*. Implies: *The house is full of whiskey and kung fu movies*. Or: *There is nowhere else to go*. Whereas AAA is scheduled to arrive in approximately three to four hours. Snow burning the shins over the brim of my socks feels good. Nowhere on a canceled Friday can be too far to walk. I'll take my words and slant through a disappeared city. Let's see if the streets burn this white, this impossible all the way home.

1. Leave-taking disorders myself at your doorstep yourself at my doorstep all night, us trading positions until your wife from a dream emerges and switches the outdoor lamps flooding on to tell us we're drowning out the crickets; holding back the sun.

   In other words, *Mercy.*

   In other words, *Fools.*

2. All the pieces were not in the box. I spent the whole afternoon attempting assemblage and deciphering Korean diagrams. Let's just get in the car, eat peaches by the open water and watch afternoon ducklings slant into bulrushes. Everything here is sunlight through my fingers, a badly translated version of something else. I cannot build a home for your blankets and spoons. Halfway there I will speak this into a car brimming saxophones and light. I will roll down the windows and let landscape peel the skin off those words.

3. I can cobble these lines anywhere, drink coffee all day, disregard instructions. I'm good at that. I search the secondhands for vinyl and needles worth scuffing the floorboards over. Soft-shoe, Foxtrot, Charleston: I could know those. And perhaps, if it came up—these rusty old springs beneath the antique sofa's patterned belly—they might be percussive, and maybe. Give it a spin. Run those songs with whiskey. All the way to dawn.

WOMAN, I AM FALLING

water; a house designed by genius, the genius
ignoring the slide rules and proportions

of his colleagues, who in turn ignore their pincurled wives,
wives with missing silk hose and seam lines penciled up

their slender calves— it was depression, is
after all, woman, there was a certain attachment to gravity

that required disruption, I promise, we needed something
impossible to believe in, an equal and opposite Cerberus hound,

in this moment of empires with slit bellies
beached amongst the shambled mewlings of other fallen

empires—woman, we needed the whole of it, jettisoned—
had to—baby and bathwater both, what a terrible thing

to be accustomed to: that casserole of lukewarm equations
— which is to say *I was dire with circumstance,*

and, since hunger nicely puts all that aside, the agency
of certain particulars, for example— I bedeviled my calculations.

Got them soused and barefoot on the Avenue of Americas.
I collected the best scrap, lipstick smiles abandoned

on champagne flutes, the sweat of bodies drunk with the proximal
stillness every city folds into, the smallest possible hours,

I promise, with every organic impulse twinkling in the rinds
of better conversation, Woman, I am Fallingwater. I am

summoned into angle and the clean lines so worth saying,
it is always worth saying, in every crucial time, in all signatures

through microphones and lacquered bells, dear: lasting is not
everything. Look at the pieces I break myself into. How otherwise

to articulate this feeling? I am trying to show you: *Onward.*
With great velocity. We beasts carrying our beast hearts within us

to the edges of the world—I am saying
how we want with everything to go.

THINGS WE KNOW ABOUT PLACES WE'VE BEEN:
A BRIEF INDEX OF YES, AND

Asphalt, The
I-95 to Plymouth and there's charcoal in your voice, closer to my ears than night sky wrapped around the car, the velvet beneath and beyond our momentum. Distance shrinking within a small vessel of space and breath. Endurance that becomes tender.

Bookstore, The
Consider the photographer Araki and his elegantly knotted women; your breath in my hair and turning pages: the way things bind. She is a young woman tied up in the gutter and pornography is the question. Her face against concrete, deeply grained but otherwise cloudless sky.

When interviewed Araki argues that ropes embrace instead of restrain; that the knots are a kind of loving. Bound in this configuration, her angles are less human—a dried hog's ear or paper crane. The rope asks that we consider the softness of wrists, the pulse throbbing there, a muted drum within mute landscape, the body as detritus among.

For days everything you see feels like Araki whispering in your ear:

We cannot help being exactly what we are.

Cargo, The
The train uneventfully moving: it wasn't serious after all, just one station after the next, platforms crowded with faces, faces not unlike my face, blankly waiting, as if for weather or any next momentary event.

We will not speak again.

Contemporary Art, The Institute of

Men for sale, languid dungarees and neutral eyes in diCorcia's gelatin print. A sun loiters above the convenience store. Leroy has a $25 asking price. We witness Des Moines, cars with rotted upholstery, asphalt edged by thirsty grass; the darkened frame beyond the blaze of Dairy Queen light. Ours is slow progress, close as moths, through the galleries. Even in the salt air outside the museum I cannot blink Leroy away.

This is a viewer's complicity with the transactions. My fingers smell guilty with money. I speak polite things with a mouth tasting of Leroy. Leroy tastes of another man's sweat, small bills in hand, still air beneath the overpass humming with mosquitos and diesel fumes.

Every photograph says: *Yes, and.*

Continent, Notes from the end of a

We stand at the ocean's crinoline skirts and watch thick swells ride up the shore, so female and runneled with salt.

She verges, collapses and rebuilds with hunger. A body of blind energy. Not like before, but now. A history swallowed like a burning thread, some bones on the floor that cannot stop dancing, cannot stop stirring in our veins.

We should go. The ocean travels where it wants.

The fistful of water through your fingers, a woman's dark hair.

Other bodies, The shores of

Our silence glitters in the sand beneath a full moon. I say Full where you say Almost. We are involved in two different arguments between

cities. We claim to be speaking of the same thing. The body under-
stands a good fit by feel, I explain, encircling the moon thumb to fin-
ger. A tongue and groove ease. Full. Almost, you said. But not quite.

Front steps, A suburban epiphany of

The low hung head. It was the beer. It was the late hour, the decid-
ing between traveling and home. Gears muddy, tongue working hard
around the words: *I am thirty one and will never have a child.* The voice
a sad, windburned animal on the doorstep.

Forgone conclusion, Sleep is a

Throw yourself as one must
so as to not to delay the shock of ice water

with all the energy we summon for such occasional things
before courage leaves us.

Harbor, Animals within the

The world outside the museum galleries remains unstaged. Late
afternoon light cloaks us in amber and slows our pace to a stroll.
Looking at art leaves us idle within ourselves, unsettled, two houses
gutted by fire and nothing left to say. It is beautiful where sky touches
us now, how it holds our thoughts in our heads and won't translate
them into English. We walk to the pier where jellyfish bloom and
crowd, their nerve centers hover in the dark water like beaded brace-
lets. They are creatures with neither brain nor heart tissue. No facility
for sensation or thought. They gather in silent hoards, small clouds
underfoot, pulsing with indifferent poison.

I, (Proof)

Can't. The room should have been an envelope, something translucent as time. Hesitation is a thing that hardens in the gullet and breaks everything that follows to bits. Consider $25 Leroy, bare-chested in his 1982 El Dorado, waiting. The waiting was not sad, but represents a decision. Consider, too, that sleep is another way of waiting. In my case, a decision not to decide. My sleep is scattered like bird seed. I sleep in bits and dashes before rising to move barefoot through the unlit house. The galleries with their bleached angles and photographs enlarged to the proportion of the lonlinesses there. The Atlantic thick with the stink and rust of algae red tide, Araki's swan-wristed women, our way of arguing over the moon. Mostly, I believe Leroy is admirable for his honest asking price. At least he knows what he is waiting for. I climb the hill to the station, old salt and the thin new sun riding heavy on my back.

Jellyfish

Begin as spores and then sprout tentacles. They are not actually fish at all. They loiter beneath the piers like badly disposed sandwich bags, and when we step from the gallery we watch. Without hearts or brains, they ingest everything in their path. *Yes, and?* They are in possession of venom but it is not personal. Why here? I touch your shoulder. The filth of Boston Harbor. Is as good a place as any.

Kindling, Your face lit by

Experience suckled from nipples and barstools, languorous back roads stretched out like sun cats between stage lights, the one by your side, breathing, or later, singing something almost familiar. Sheets or body like a wick, lain. Lit.

Knots, Sageo

Bindings used to secure swords upon the hips of Kendo warriors. The Obi, prized for its beauty and effectiveness, knots up the front or is knotted double around back. It is an old way, predating even the butterfly knot. This makes a different riddle of the woman in the street. She is a weapon prepared, beautifully secured to landscape. This Japan is sleepy concrete fury with radioactive eyes. Breath entering and reentering the Ota River, a soup of bones and constant screaming, the city a street fighter with an elegant weapon strapped to its hip.

Outside, Inside

As good a place as any, a garage sale in the middle of the block on the way out of town. This is how you know you're leaving: a stoop lined with vinyl records where the sellers watch you examine cover art. You stop because it is the only thing keeping you. Commodores. DeBarge. Isley Brothers. We used to have big ideas and pants that cut the human profile on a bias. Shirt collars like fighter jet wings. It was about angularity and tensions. *Just looking* you say to the seller's blank face. *How much is this?* Your attention gives sudden value to the items, and his conflict is a loud unspoken thing. Were his wife not on the porch with her hard-boiled eyes. Were the catalytic converter not toasted. And were there not such years of it—aluminum siding, canned peas—he might smuggle that vinyl back inside to reshelve within a trunk full of gold hits from bebop to disco to neosoul. You understand this dilemma and hand him the record. Having loved disco. Dolly Parton. Donna Summer. Teased hair and lamé. He is disappointed and pleased with equal measure. It is your ticket home, not buying the album. A near exact exchange. A block away you buy the tallest coffee on earth and step on your shadow the whole way to the train station. You are surprised to find you know the way without trying. But then, you knew from the beginning exactly where you were.

Of course it was a full moon.

Poker face
You do not want to wake up and put your work trousers on, did not. Never do. It is part of your charm. I was hoping you might telephone, but took the first train I knew I could catch. Exhaustion is the weight of another man on your back, badly carried. Sleep arrived like a kind of revenge as soon as I was comfortably gone. I finished the coffee and found myself in Boston with a stiff neck. The ocean in the shells I stole from the beach. A knot of nerves, a single ring of thought, pinched by sleep.

Providence
When I rose it was already hot. The blinds opened whips of fire, desperate for something to cut through stale cigarettes, vague mildew. Puppies. Coffee. Skin.

Tall ships, The traffic of
Past the bridge a standstill, taillights zipped up interstate, where I wandered between bumpers, exhaust on my ankles between cars, hotly idled. The moon was full. An impossibly full, cardboard, variety show moon. Full and low. Close enough to scrape—but that didn't seem possible, either. My brightness amplified by headlights; an ocean nearby but not within sight. Something so large and close and undetected. Impossible. Nothing is.

Until full, Birds sing

Birds sing because they are male and want to say so. My nest. My ladybird. *Mine.* The singing lays them vulnerable to predators, locates them. They cannot hear the danger coming while singing their lot. They cannot guarantee their lot without singing. Risk is beautiful music. In my trees they start boasting at 4:30 a.m. Your dream breath is thick and steady counterpoint. Not claiming. Not moving forward, but with.

LET US STAY

Let there be soft space in the outcome,
a possibility we might overgrow our borders,

become whole counties of light. Let us remember
this season, our chins tucked, our hard lean

into gray wind. Let the heart go rich with moss.
Let it have no footprints. Let the sun bleach

the bones of words you no longer need.
Let the birds sing in orange and red.

Let the underfoot miles go. Let everything you touch
name you. Let it be a long kiss. Let us stay

until Sirius skips his scorched heart like a stone
through the last spokes of darkness.

A lump of girl in square coal interiors (a box within a box within a box). A pandemonium of velvet striping, swelter and balm, such good. Oscillating and muscled thick. Torn dungarees, edged by corn-field, by heat lightning. *Let's get gone* portly for hops, for lateness and sound check. A smile breaking open. A soft new sorry. (A box un-locked, opening unto another box.) Feels like progress. Stir of an old song, sways across the room, a voice slow as late summer honeybees, moving from one sticky flower to the next. Let me. Show you. This trustworthy voice in a field after dark. Gold there. *Did you see?*

ACKNOWLEDGMENTS

"Girl #1," "Girl #2," "Fall," and "Devoted" appeared in the *Carolina Quarterly*; "Gig" appeared in *32 poems*; "Elements" appeared in *Salt Hill* and the 2004 Cave Canem anthology; "Chaser" appeared in *Salt Hill*; and "Welcome Home" appeared in *Ploughshares*.

I am thankful for the keenness and generosity of the following people whose feedback and encouragement helped build these poems: Michael Coppola, Victoria Bosch Murray, Michael Lynch, Prabakar Thyagarajan, Neil Callender, John Edgar Wideman, Bernard Matambo, Mike Kim, Daniel C. Howe, Ryan C. Daley, Aya Karpinska, Brianna Colburn, Caroline Whitbeck, Kate Shapira, Tasha C. Miller, Surekha Samal, Major Jackson, L'Merchie Frazier, Rebecca J. Spencer, Michael Harris, Claudia Rankine, Terrance Hayes, Thomas Sayers Ellis, Sopheap Pich, Theresa Gaignard, Tom Daley, Nate Van Til, Regie O'Hare Gibson, Carole Maso, Keith Waldrop, Toi Derricotte, Patricia Smith, and Diana, Edward, Lisa, and Eddie Dutton.

Many thanks to the Fine Arts Work Center in Provincetown, Cave Canem Foundation, Virginia Center for the Creative Arts, and Brown University, all of which provided resources that allowed these poems to be written.

Lastly, my thanks to Brad Barr, Andrew Barr, and Marc Friedman of The Slip for both title and, of course, the music.